Lindemann Group

Peter Schiessl

MAIL MERGE
WITH MICROSOFT
WORD 2019
Training book with Exercises

ISBN 979-8-709583-85-6
Translated into English by Peter Schiessl
V241103 / Lindemann Group
Publisher: Lindemann BHIT, Munich
Postal address: LE/Schiessl, Fortnerstr. 8, 80933 Munich, Germany
E-Mail: post@kamiprint.de / Telefax: 0049 (0)89 99 95 46 83
© MSc. (UAS) Peter Schiessl, Munich, Germany
www.lindemann-beer.com / www.kamiprint.de

REQUEST EXERCISE TEXTS FOR THIS BOOK BY EMAIL: post@kamiprint.de

Table of Contents

1. Preface

The structure of this three-part book series should enable you to learn MS Word excellently and step by step without the usual frustration experiences.

You have already seen in the first volume that many things are possible with Word, such as WordArt, Tables, and Tabs or the different Colors for Text or Frames. This training has to be especially systematic because Word offers so many possibilities.

1.1 The three steps to Wordiness

1st Book	2nd Book	3rd Book
Introduction to Word Operation and Program structure, Basic word processing (Font and Paragraph settings), Text design with frames, Color, Numbering and Enumerations, Tabs and Tables, Spell checking, Hyphenation, WordArt …	An advanced word processor with Style sheets, Headers, Footnotes, Table of Contents, Basic deepening, Drawing, Insert graphics, Tables, Search and Replace, Business cards, Serial letters, and Labels.	Word for specialists: Different Headers or Footers in one Text, Table of Contents, Index, Automatic Numbering, Create your own Dictionaries, Efficient Working with Shortcuts, Sentence Basics, Split Large Documents, More Macros …
Course objective: To make short texts appealing, e.g. a business letter or a birthday invitation.	Course objective: Longer texts can be effectively edited and designed, e.g. an annual report or a three-column circular.	Course objective: Perfectly design Brochures, Presentations or Doctoral Theses with Index and different Headers.

Please note our special editions:

♦ Serial letters/labels*. The respective material was compiled from volumes 2 and 3 and expanded by additional exercises.

♦ How to create Websites with Word is described in our book "Creating a Homepage with MS Word XX"[1].

---

[1] Currently sold out, if new available, the books are offered on www.amazon.com

1.2 About this Volume

♦ Text processing for advanced users means that extensive texts are processed. The most important topics of this volume are therefore

↳ the style sheets as an indispensable basis for formatting (=adjusting) longer texts. In addition, an automatic table of contents can only be generated using style sheets.

♦ For the daily use, it is worthwhile to individually adjust Word, e.g. add new symbols or adjust the automatic saving or the intended storage location, etc.

♦ And then, of course, there are the practical functions that are essential for professional documents:

↳ Automatically create Table of Contents, set Headers, automatic Page Numbering, Footnotes, Source References, a Macro, Serial Letters, Labels, etc.

In this book, more is described than can be done in a course. Style sheets, Headers and Footers, Footnotes and Endnotes, Cross-references and Serial Letters/Labels should be the basic framework.

1.3 Test your knowledge

Answer the following questions so that you know which course or book is best for you:

♦ Can you write a business letter and set the font and size? Have you ever placed a paragraph in a frame or changed the text color? Do you have any problems with tables and tabs?

↳ These basics are covered in Volume 1. If you have mastered these functions, then Volume 2 is the right choice for you.

♦ Can you reformat a multi-page text with style sheets? Have you already successfully created and adopted a table of contents? Are you familiar with Footnotes and Endnotes, Search and Replace, how to insert graphics, and how to customize toolbars?

↳ Then Volume 3 will be very interesting for you.

REQUEST EXERCISE TEXTS FOR THIS BOOK BY EMAIL: post@kamiprint.de

2. Serial Letters

Afraid of serial letters? Not anymore longer. We can open an existing document which should then become our serial letter or start the mail merge function and create a new letter or select an existing letter from the mail merge menu.

2.1 As an Illustration

With serial printing, you do not manually put an address in a letter for printing. Instead, you have a letter in which addresses are automatically inserted from a database.

It doesn't matter whether it is a letter, an email or an envelope, or whether you want to create a new database or use an existing one.

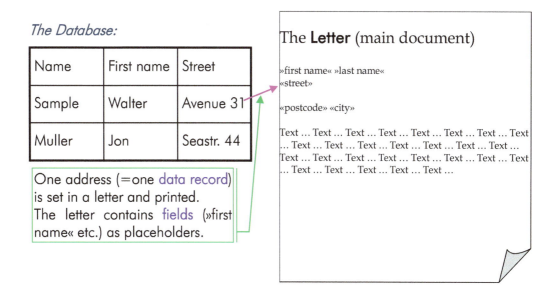

The Database:

Name	First name	Street
Sample	Walter	Avenue 31
Muller	Jon	Seastr. 44

One address (=one data record) is set in a letter and printed. The letter contains fields (»first name« etc.) as placeholders.

The **Letter** (main document)

»first name« »last name«
«street»

«postcode» «city»

Text ... Text ...

Therefore, these three steps must be carried out one after the other:

♦ The actual serial letter (or envelope etc.),

♦ then the data source with the addresses must be created or opened,

   ✎ Fields in the main document specify where each data from the data source is to be inserted,

♦ and finally, the actual action can be started as often as you like, in which an address is placed in a letter and printed.

2.2 A business letter

We will first create a practice letter to make it clearer. Since serial letters are almost always of a business nature and are produced in large quantities, it is a good idea to design a letter in accordance with the standards. Actual standards you find e.g. in Wikipedia, search for business letter.

2.2.1 Page Setup (Layout/Page Setup)

♦ In a new document, all margins should be between 1 and 1 1/4 inch.

   ↳ You can enter the Letterhead in the header line to protect it from unintentional changes.

   ↳ Then you would enter 2 inch as the top margin for the sender and ¾ inch for the header on the Layout tab, but it depends how many lines and how big you want your letterhead.

   ↳ The U.S. paper size is 8.5 x 11 inch = 216 x 279 cm.

➢ Enter a letterhead in the header line:

   ↳ This sender address can be freely designed and also embellished with WordArt.

   ↳ Add a logo, e.g. via WordArt.

> My Example Ltd.
> Work street 1
> 01234 Big City
> www.myexample.com
> email@myexymple.com

2.2.2 The Address

The address with the sender's details should fit well into the viewing window, although in the case of business mail merge documents, it should be noted that as a rule, there are many addresses with additional lines, such as the company address or department. Therefore, it is better to start at the top of the envelope window and do not select a too large font.

♦ The position of the adress block: Measure the viewing window from your usual envelope, then apply this measure for the address block in the mailing list.

♦ Use a small font and a dividing line to indicate the sender address above the address area, so that the letter can return if necessary.

The correct Address:[2]

To one person:	To a Company:
1. Annotations, e.g. Personal	1. Annotations and Additions, e.g. Personal
2. Annotations, e.g. Personal	2. Annotations and Additions, e.g. Personal
3. e.g. Registered mail	3. Form of dispatch, e.g. by registered mail
4.	4. Company
5.Salutation, Title	5. Salutation
6.First name Surname	6. Contact person
7. Street	7. Street, P.O. Box
8. Postcode and City	8. Postcode and City
9. Country	9. Country

---

[2] Address formats by country and area: https://en.wikipedia.org/wiki/Address

2.2.3 A Specimen Letter

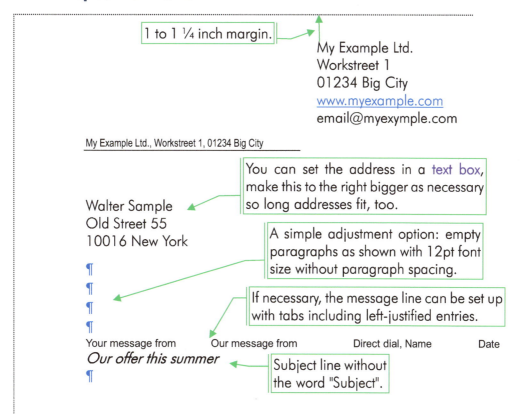

> ➤ The message line is followed by the subject line, but the word subject is currently no longer written.

> ➤ Before the text of the letter, write the salutation "Dear Ladies, Dear Gentlemen," and at the end "With kind regards".

>> ↳ Obviously, better than this impersonal address is: "Dear Mr. Anton Receiver". Such differentiated salutations followed in the third volume in the query conditions for serial letters.

Dear Madam,
Dear Sir,

   ¶

----This is where the letter text begins.----

> ➤ At the bottom of the page, preferably in the footer, enter some more details including the bank details in the footer of a business letter.

>> ↳ With a centered and a right-aligned tab, everything can be arranged as shown.

Phone:111 12345678-12	My bank	Management: Anton Example
Telefax:111 12345678-9	Account-No. 11111	AG New York HRB 11111
email@myexample.com	SORT CODE 111 111 11	VAT ID No. DE0000 111 111
www.myexample.com	IBAN: 1234 1234 1234 1234 1234 12	Tax No. 345/234XX

> ➤ Simply save this letter to a folder called "Letters", then open this letter later and with Save file as open, customize and save under a suitable file name. This is more convenient than creating a document template.

2.3 Create the Data Source

Let's start converting the letter into a serial print document.

➤ First delete the sample adress and set the cursor at this place.

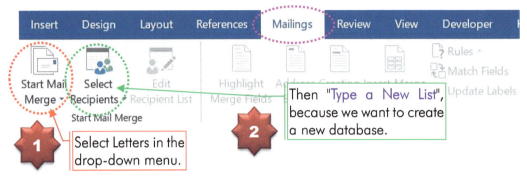

◆ In the drop-down list, you can see, that emails, envelopes, labels, etc. can also be created as serial documents, e.g., to print addresses directly onto envelopes.

◆ You can select an existing database as the data source instead of creating a new data list.

An input window for the first data is displayed:

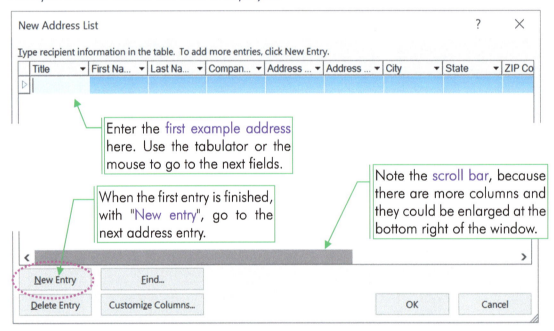

For example, enter these three sample addresses:

Title	First Name	Last Name	Address line 1	ZIP CODE	City	Work Phone
Mr.	Walter	Sample	Old Street 55	10016	New York	345 3435 3435
Ms.	Antonia	Muller	Backerstr. 32	8888	Detroit	
Mr.	Sam	Smith	Main Street 1	90013	Los Angeles	

Let's use the given fields to avoid too much at the beginning. We will explain later on page 95 how to rename, delete or add new fields.

2.3.1 Save database

If you press "Close", the database is automatically saved.

> ➢ The save window appears, save the database in our exercise folder letters with the filename "SampleAddressList".

2.4 Edit Data Source

We should now practice how to reopen the database to include more records or correct errors.

Edit
Recipient List

♦ Although the database is saved in MS Access format mdb, it can still be further processed in MS Word.

➢ Select "Edit Recipient List",

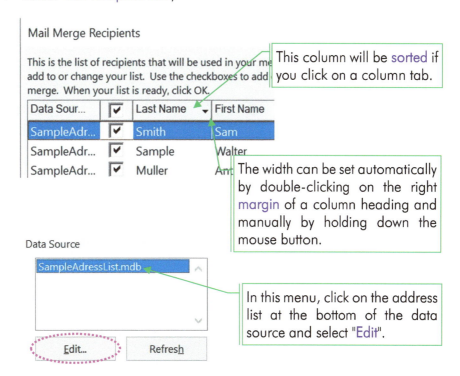

Mail Merge Recipients

This is the list of recipients that will be used in your me[rge]. add to or change your list. Use the checkboxes to add [to] you merge. When your list is ready, click OK.

Data Sour...	☑	Last Name ▾	First Name
SampleAdr...	☑	Smith	Sam
SampleAdr...	☑	Sample	Walter
SampleAdr...	☑	Muller	An[t...]

This column will be sorted if you click on a column tab.

The width can be set automatically by double-clicking on the right margin of a column heading and manually by holding down the mouse button.

Data Source

SampleAdressList.mdb

Edit...   Refresh

In this menu, click on the address list at the bottom of the data source and select "Edit".

> ➢ Enter additional addresses for the exercise:

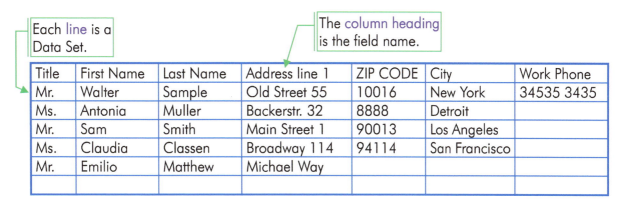

Each line is a Data Set.

The column heading is the field name.

Title	First Name	Last Name	Address line 1	ZIP CODE	City	Work Phone
Mr.	Walter	Sample	Old Street 55	10016	New York	34535 3435
Ms.	Antonia	Muller	Backerstr. 32	8888	Detroit	
Mr.	Sam	Smith	Main Street 1	90013	Los Angeles	
Ms.	Claudia	Classen	Broadway 114	94114	San Francisco	
Mr.	Emilio	Matthew	Michael Way			

2.4.1 Edit new Fields and Fields

In the previous menu, you can not only add new fields but also rename, delete or optimize the sequence of existing fields under "Customize columns":

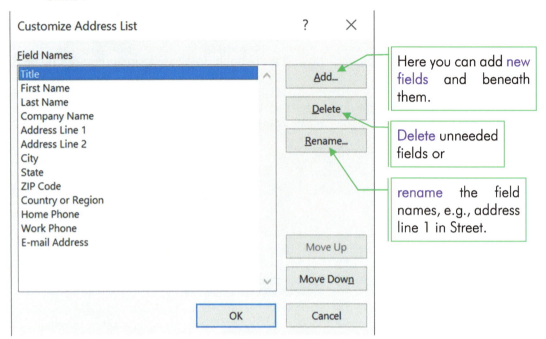

> ➤ After the salutation, add a new Title field and rename address line 1 to Street, address line 2 to No. (a dot does not work as a field name) and correct the entries.

> ➤ Change the order of the fields meaningfully, e.g. cash on delivery first, then salutation, title, first name, etc.

> ♦ is not that hard to remember, because F7 is the spellchecker.

Notes: ....

....

....

....

....

....

....

....

....

....

....

3. Complete Mail Merge

Then you can return to the mail merge and set up the mail merge. Word can be used to do this, e.g. by inserting the address block or the salutation completely formatted.

> ➤ First, place the cursor on the desired position, then you can

> ✎ prefabricated address block

> ✎ or select a greeting line (Dear ...)

> ✎ or arrange the fields for the address itself appropriately (insert Merge Field).

The Address Block:

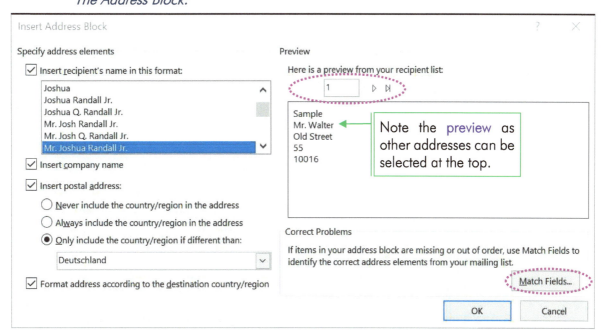

No matter which defaults setting you chose on the left, the finished address blocks are not always optimal, so we are going to practice creating the address ourselves.

> ➤ Select the Address Block/Choose Match Fields...

> ➤ As shown on the next page, you must select the correct fields on the right for the address to be displayed correctly.

The fields must be filled-in appropriately:

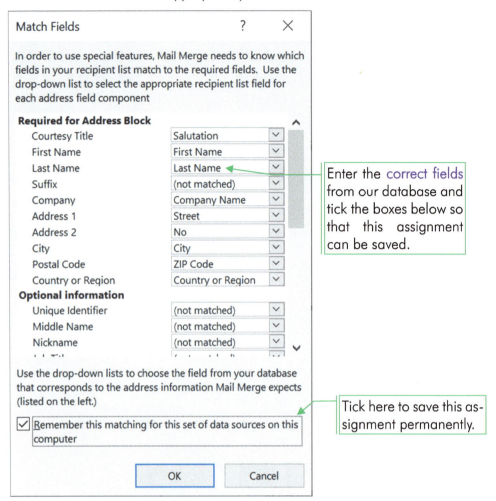

Enter the correct fields from our database and tick the boxes below so that this assignment can be saved.

Tick here to save this assignment permanently.

This will be done in the serial document after OK:

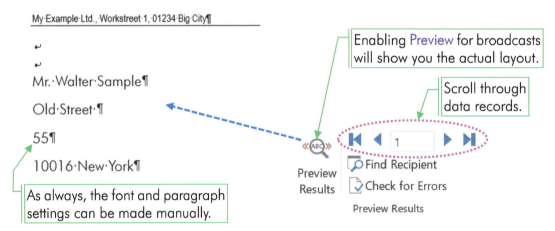

Enabling Preview for broadcasts will show you the actual layout.

Scroll through data records.

As always, the font and paragraph settings can be made manually.

Preview Results

> The font and paragraph settings can be made manually as usual. Format: Postcode and City in bold with 14 pt font size.

The completed address block and greeting line, therefore, require some adjustments until everything fits as desired so that it is usually easier to manually compile the address.

> Obviously, for comparison and practice, you can insert the address block and then manually arrange the fields below it again using the following procedure.

3.1 Set up Address and Fields

The address block does not necessarily save work, it is often easier to manually compile an address. In this way, all existing data in the serial document can be used anywhere in the document, e.g. to find out whether a telephone number is still correct.

Delete address blocks and compile an address manually:

➢ Close the mail merge window with the X symbol, delete the inserted address, then move the cursor to the address position in the letter.

➢ Press the "Insert Merge Field" icon (or "More Items" from the wizard), then select the first "Salutation" field.

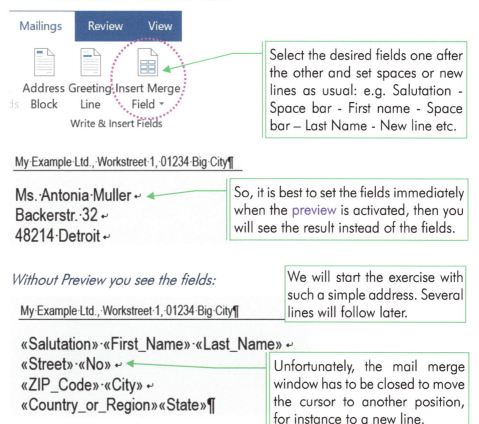

Select the desired fields one after the other and set spaces or new lines as usual: e.g. Salutation - Space bar - First name - Space bar – Last Name - New line etc.

So, it is best to set the fields immediately when the preview is activated, then you will see the result instead of the fields.

Without Preview you see the fields:

We will start the exercise with such a simple address. Several lines will follow later.

Unfortunately, the mail merge window has to be closed to move the cursor to another position, for instance to a new line.

3.1.1 Worth knowing about Fields

♦ Fields, e.g., «Surname»: You only have to set the fields as if they were a correct address.

♦ You can treat fields like normal text, i.e. select, format or even cut them and paste them elsewhere.

↳ The only important thing is that you always take the «»-field characters with you.

♦ If you select a field, such as »Postal code«, and set a larger font, this applies to all postal codes of mail merge.

Fields are placeholders: the last name from the database is inserted in the Last Name field, the street in the Street field, and so on. A related address is a data set.

3.2 Start Mail Merge

Finally, all that remains is to execute the mail merge. An address is inserted into a letter and printed, automatically followed by the next address, and so on. (=connecting the addresses with the letter).

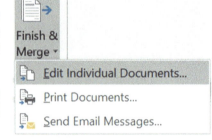

➢ Always check with the preview function first.
  At least some addresses should be checked.

➢ Then start the mail merge by "Finish & Merge", preferably with "edit individual documents" into a new, normal Word document, which you can then view for checking before printing.

    ↳ This is also a practical method to print only certain addresses. Search for these pages and enter the page numbers in the print menu.

    ↳ You can also save this new mail merge document so that you can print individual letters from it again later.

♦ Edit Individual Documents...:

    ↳ It does not print but creates a new text that you can look at for review.

    ↳ Do not correct here, but always in the original letter, then restart the mail merge.

    ↳ As a rule, this document should not be saved, since you can recreate it at any time.

> Good for checking, because errors are always noticeable.

♦ Print documents: every serial letter will be printed immediately.

    ↳ Usually, you notice some impossible errors after thirty pages and start over, so it takes longer than if you first printed into a document for checking.

♦ With the last option, send e-mail messages...,

    ↳ serial e-mails would be generated instead of serial letters,

    ↳ the data source must, of course, contain email addresses and "Close" must be selected in the following window.

> If you start offline your Email-software can't send, so you can check a last time the finished Emails.

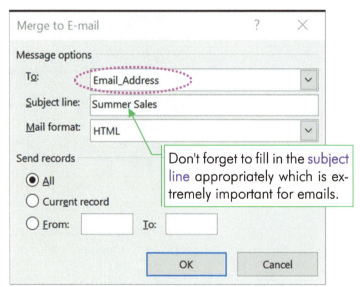

Don't forget to fill in the subject line appropriately which is extremely important for emails.

3.3 Tips for large Mail Merge-Actions

To be Corrected:

- ◆ Not only view the preview on screen, but also print at least one data set.

  - ✎ Correct this printout thoroughly, because the frustration and loss of time are enormous when hundreds of serial letters have been printed that have to be sent to the waste paper because of small errors!

> Always correct with a sharp printout on paper with time. The display on the screen is significantly worse so that errors that are immediately noticeable on the paper printout are overlooked!

- ◆ The person who created the letter must never be the only one who proofreads it.

  - ✎ At least one, preferably two other persons should proofread without time pressure.

  - ✎ Own mistakes are mostly overlooked, no matter how often the text is read!

To Print:

- ◆ Printing can take a long time, especially if you have used images or lines.

  - ✎ When the computer prints for twenty minutes, then crashes, the tedious search begins to identify which address was last printed.

- ◆ This is a bit easier if you print in stages and sorted into a new document (e.g. postal code from 80000 to 85000).

How does it work?

- ◆ The simplest method is to print a new document, save it and then enter the desired page numbers when printing.

  - ✎ In this document, letters that have already been printed can be deleted if necessary.

- ◆ Another way is via the filters, which are explained in the third volume on MS Word and in this Special Edition on Serial Letters and Labels.

Simulate an emergency:

When sending as email, the format is converted into HTML format, i.e. something can definitely shift or change. Almost nothing is a bigger disaster than emailing incorrect messages to customers or business partners, especially if it were several hundred or thousands.

> If you disconnect your computer from the Internet (disconnect the WLAN connection, switch off the router or disconnect the network cable), you can have the serial emails created in real life, but since nothing can be sent, you can check them again at your leisure.

3.4 Database as MS Word Table

If you would rather have a database than a normal table in an MS Word document, as was the case with previous Word versions, this is also possible with the following trick.

> ➢ Select "New document". Create a table in this new document.
>
>> ✎ In this table, the column headings are entered in the first line. The field names are entered later.
>>
>> ✎ Important: this table may only exist, no paragraphs in front of the table!

Accept an existing MS Word data table:

If the data table has already been created, you can also select it in the mail merge wizard or for an existing mail merge document using the button shown.

Select
Recipients ▾

Edit a Word Data Table:

If you use a Word document with a table as the data source, it is easier to edit or print it in Word.

- ◆ Simply open this document to edit a Word data table. In this table, you can work like in any other table:

  - ✎ Add new Lines (=Datasets),

  - ✎ Delete Lines, Change Data, etc.

  - ✎ You can even use all table tools to make the table more beautiful and possibly printable.

- ◆ You can also insert a new field in the database language by entering the name of the new field in the first line of the column.

- ◆ You can also change field names (= column headers).

  - ✎ Delete the old field name and insert it again if the field is already used in a document.

- ◆ Landscape format is suitable for printing which can be selected for page layout orientation.

Note: ....
....
....
....
....
....
....
....
....
....
....
....
....

4. Create Labels

- ♦ We merged a data set with a letter in the mail merge.

  - ✎ The data sets for labels are only put together differently and exactly match the label stickers.

- ♦ Usually, you only need to specify the type of label you are using because all standard label formats are already saved in Word.

  - ✎ The cumbersome work of adapting the printout to the labels is no longer necessary.

4.1 Using the Mail Merge Wizard

We want to put an address from our database on a label and therefore start this time with the serial print wizard.

- ➤ Start a new, blank Document.

- ➤ Use the "Step by Step Mail merge wizard" tab with Start mail merge tab.

Start Mail Merge ▾

Choose Labels this time. ───→

Mail Merge ▾ ✕

Select document type

What type of document are you working on?

- ● Letters
- ○ E-mail messages
- ○ Envelopes
- ○ Labels
- ○ Directory

Letters

Send letters to a group of people. You can personalize the letter that each person receives.

Click Next to continue.

- ➤ After Next, you can select the label form under "Label options":

Change document layout

Click Label options to choose a label size.

▤ Label options...

Step 1 of 6

→ Next: Starting document

4.2 Select Label Format

You can select the label formats from almost all label manufacturers in the following menu under Label Options. This means the label form is already perfectly set up.

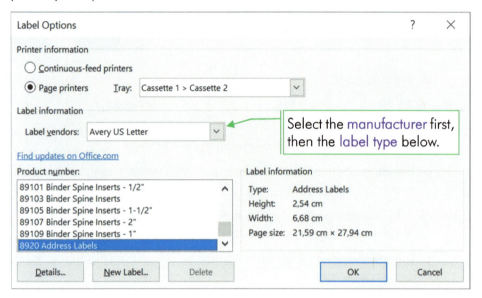

- ♦ The label dimensions can be displayed for checking under Details. You can also change the dimensions in this menu.

- ♦ A format can be set manually for "New label". This involves a lot of work!

4.3 Select the Data Source

➢ We want to use the data source we created in the last exercise, so after "Next... " "Use an existing list."

➢ and with Browse, the database created during the previous mail merge exercise and confirm all data.

✎ You can use the checkmarks to select specific addresses in case not all of them are desired.

➢ After "Next..." the addresses can be placed on the labels.

Set up the Document:

- ➢ Add the address block to the first label (correct the order of the fields in "Set Matching Fields").

- ➢ To print the next address on each label, press the "Update all labels" button.

  - ↳ You can also use this button to apply formatting or field composition changes to all other labels.

- ➢ Use the preview (Next...) to check and then print it out in a new document.

That's the way it has to be. Insert «Address block» in the first field, «Next Record» and «Address block» in the next field so that the next address will be printed:

««Address»»	«Next Record» «AddressBlock»	«Next Record» «AddressBlock»
«Next Record» «AddressBlock»	«Next Record» «AddressBlock»	«Next Record» «AddressBlock»
«Next Record» «AddressBlock»	«Next Record» «AddressBlock»	«Next Record» «AddressBlock»

- ➢ Now the label is set up and you can print or save the label sheet.

- ➢ But the number is again in a new line. Delete all and arrange with "Insert Merge Fields" one address manually, copy them in next labels and "Update Labels". I found its manually easier and match as you want.

4.4 Save Labels

- ➢ With "Previous..." you can go back and make changes at any time or format the address block differently, e.g. centered or insert an upper paragraph spacing.

The work should be saved when everything is perfectly set up:

- ➢ Select Save as normal for this function.

  - ↳ Do not save a printout to a file because you can re-create it at any time, but save the label sheet!

  - ↳ It is advisable to assign the label number as the file name.

  - ↳ If you save all labels together in one folder, you will find them again without any problems.

There is no need to re-set the labels each time, you only need to open the saved file.

4.5 Envelopes and individual Labels

So far, we've handled the mail merge. Serial printing saves a lot of work e.g. with circulars to all club members or to create advertising mailings.

4.5.1 Envelope or Label

Sometimes only a single letter should be printed, for example to a new member of the association.

- ♦ either you use an envelope with a viewing window and put your return address very small over the address, as we did with our exercise letter, or

- ♦ you can print individual labels or a single envelope without having to write the address twice. Good for envelopes without viewing window.

4.5.2 Select an Address

- ♦ You can return to the serial print commands at any time on the Mailings tab.

Edit
Recipient List

- ♦ In "Edit recipient list" you can only tick the desired data set:

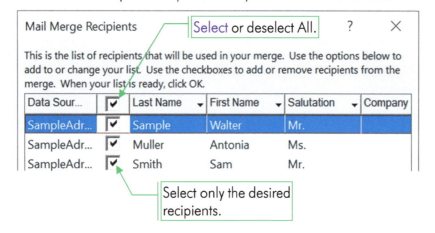

- ♦ With "Finish & Merge" you can also select which data set is to be printed.

Finish &
Merge ▾

Finish

If you do not want to print a label in the upper left corner, e.g. in order to consume a label sheet bit by bit, simply crop the address in the preview and insert it at the desired label position.

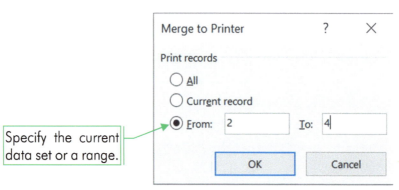

4.6 Envelopes

4.6.1 Envelope Handmade

The simple practical solution for printed envelopes is to set up the envelope as a normal file:

♦ for example, use your envelopes paper format without a window and place the address in a document with same size as envelope in a text box (Insert/Text Box) so that it can be moved easily or the address paragraph can be moved to the desired position.

♦ For preset letters File/New and then search for "Envelopes".

♦ The address will be copied from the letter and inserted into the envelope, then if necessary save the envelope for later use with "Save as" in a separate "Envelopes" folder.

    ✎ In the same way, you can equip an envelope document set up in this way with mail merge fields instead of a specific address in order to print envelopes directly from the database.

4.6.2 The Envelope Print-function

This Word function is available instead of the manual work described above:

➢ You could first open a finished letter, select the address and copy it, then select Envelopes on the Mailings tab and paste the previously copied address using the following menu.

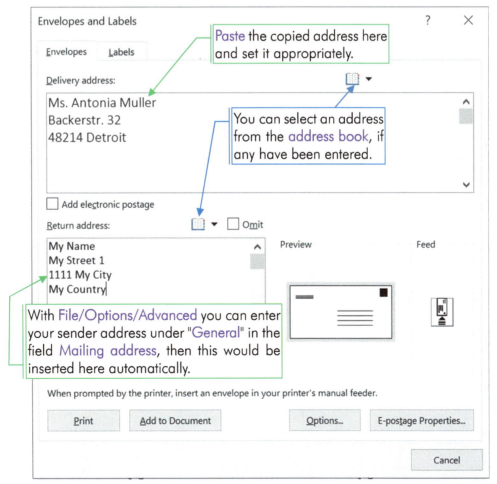

♦ Observe the preview on which you can also click, e.g. to specify the position of the address field when printing in a menu.

♦ Various envelopes and label formats can be selected for options.

♦ Use the Envelopes tab for envelopes, the Labels tab for label changes or the Labels button:

> With "Add to Document" you print in a new document, in this you can check or arrange again before real printing.

4.7 Print Business Cards

It is also possible to create business cards if labels can already be printed. The graphic possibilities of Word are amazing.

Perfect cards can be created with colored pre-printed business cards which can be easily separated by a perforation. Measure the cards and use similar labels, especially those of the same height if there is no template.

➤ Start a new, blank document. The simplest way to print such cards is the command discussed earlier for mailing-envelopes:

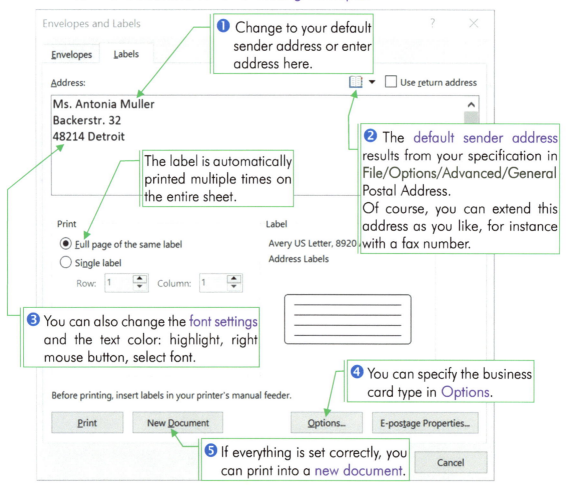

You will receive a text that you can finally save and format as described in the next section.

4.7.1 Design Business Cards

Resize:

With the prefabricated cards, you only need to specify the type again. If you cut your own cards or if the type is not available, either select a suitable standard type or set the label manually.

You receive a table filled with your data. The table commands allow you to adjust the format very easily afterward.

➢ Make a test printout on smear paper and place over the business card paper.

Adjust the columns and rows of the table manually until everything fits:

➢ Select row or column, right mouse button and enter an exact value for table properties. Systematically compare test printouts to get closer to the original.

➢ If the table size fits your business card paper, you can save it as a template for further work.

➢ If you want to create a new business card, access it and only exchange the entry, such as a new phone number, with the Replace at start command.

Change Design:

Secondly, the text of the business card should be optimized. The way to recreate the label template is much more cumbersome than the following:

➢ Make the first label appealing:

↳ Use all your knowledge, e.g. font size, color, italic or bold, text inverted or embellished with WordArt, small caps, locked, line spacing, special characters, graphic elements such as lines or triangles, etc.

➢ Finally, select this one label, copy it with [Ctrl]-c and paste it into the other fields with [Ctrl]-v.

Only copy when everything really fits! This only becomes apparent after a test printout.

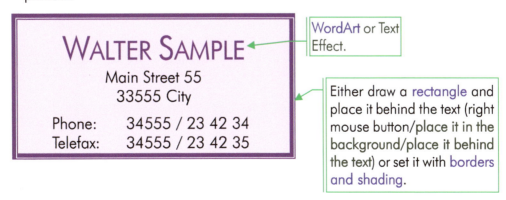

WalterSample

Main Street 55
33555 City

Phone: 34555 / 23 42 34
Telefax: 34555 / 23 42 35

WordArt or Text Effect.

Either draw a rectangle and place it behind the text (right mouse button/place it in the background/place it behind the text) or set it with borders and shading.

5. Special Serial Letter

With query conditions, serial letters can be individually designed and adapted to the characteristics of the origin language.

- ♦ For example, the American spelling "City, State Postal Code" could be replaced by English: "City" and in new line "postal code" if recipient is from Great Britain.
  - ↳ Or it can be determined that a special invoice address is used. If there is no billing address, the usual address will still appear in the letterhead.

Word moves here in a border area to database programs. And therefore, you have to consider whether it would not be better to use a database program from the outset. A decision support:

WORD	DATABASE, E.G. ACCESS
Easy handling of the text editing and good design options for the serial letters (WordArt, drawing).	Limited text editing, but serial letters can be created with graphic elements and calculations.
No double training in two programs.	Additional knowledge of the database program required.
Too slow for large amounts of data.	Designed for large data volumes.
The data cannot be distributed over several small databases.	Relational database: several small databases are linked together.

- ♦ Word is suitable for text editing with a limited amount of data, e.g., for the circulars or advertising letters in a club or a smaller company.
- ♦ However, if you have large amounts of data (over 10,000 data saves) to manage, Word reaches its limits with simple database programs without the possibility of relational databases.

Nevertheless, you will be amazed at what is possible in Word.

5.1 Create a Serial Letter

The best exercise for the practice is an exercise from the practice: Let's create an invoice as a serial letter.

Why even an invoice, a single sheet as a serial letter?

♦ So that the address does not have to be rewritten or copied.

♦ If additional pages are added to this serial letter (one page for delivery bill, one page for a new order form), the invoice can be extended with these pages and you have with one action some documents ready.

    ✎ Thus, the address does not need to be written some times, but it is sufficient to enter the customer number once as a query condition, and all necessary documents are ready.

Furthermore, we do not need to know whether another billing address exists for this customer, because if this is set correctly in the database, the billing address is automatically entered, if it exists in the database.

➢ Open the text InvoiceExercise.doc. Confirm the security message that an SQL command will be started with Yes and save it as a copy in your exercise folder.

> SQL means structured query language, a programming language for work with databases, since 1986 declared as the standard database language by ANSI and 1987 by ISO.

5.2 Address in a Text Field

We start with the delivery bill. We could now enter the mail merge fields for the address.

♦ Problem: if a line is left blank or an address is very long, the rest of the text moves, which can totally mess up a long mail merge document.

♦ To avoid this, we put the address in a text box.

    ✎ The size of this text field is fixed.

    ✎ This ensures that the remaining text is independent of the number of lines in the address.

Unintentional blank pages or inappropriate page layout are thus reliably prevented.

➢ First save the template in your exercise folder with File/Save as, and change the file name, e.g., in Invoice -my exercise, to avoid confusion.

➢ Insert a text field for the address below the header (Insert/Text field)

➢ and set this: Text wrap "in front of text", so you can copy ore move easier the merge fields in this box, with other variants, word selects the text paragraphs outside the text frame rather than target when inserting, and turn off the line (no outline).

5.3 To the Mail Merge Document

Our text must now be extended to a mail merge document. You already know this from volume 2:

➢ In order not to change the example database "SampleCustomers", copy it into your exercise folder first,

➢ then on the Mailings tab, choose by "Select Recipients" "Use Existing List", open the database SampleCustomers.doc as data source from your exercises folder and click on the

➢ "Insert merge field" and set the fields for the address in the text box.

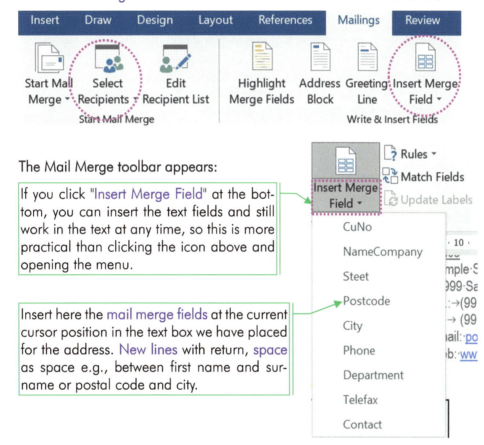

The Mail Merge toolbar appears:

If you click "Insert Merge Field" at the bottom, you can insert the text fields and still work in the text at any time, so this is more practical than clicking the icon above and opening the menu.

Insert here the mail merge fields at the current cursor position in the text box we have placed for the address. New lines with return, space as space e.g., between first name and surname or postal code and city.

Empty lines

Empty lines: empty lines are omitted if Return was used at the end of the line, with "New Line" (Shift + Return), empty lines will definitely remain. Unfortunately, this only works for simple fields, no longer if if-then conditions are built in.

This is how the address block could be:

«Contact» «Department» «NameCompany» «Street» «City», «Postcode»	A very wide text field to accommodate long names. Since the manual insertion of the fields is very easy, we do not need to deal with the prefabricated and mostly not optimally fitting compilations at "Address Block".

You can set the text fields all at once and then arrange them with Return and punctuation marks or one after the other in the correct position.

5.4 Check with the Preview

Unfortunately, some adjustments are still needed until a perfect mail merge document is created, so we should check the result more often.

➢ Activate the preview on the Shipments tab, then go through the pages and check them.

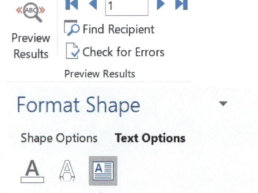

➢ First problem, the text field is automatically adjusted to the existing lines. This should be turned off if you change the size manually, i.e., set it a bit higher.

↳ If it is still on, right-click on the text field and "Format Shape" check in Text Options/Layout and Properties that "Resize shape to fit text" is disabled. If necessary, increase the height of the text field again manually.

➢ In this menu you can also set the inner edges of the frame to be 0.1mm everywhere.

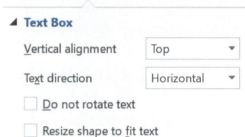

5.5 First condition If-Then-Else

In American usage, the postcode is placed after the city after a comma; we want to use this as our standard. For an address from United Kingdom, we would like to adapt the address output as usual in Great Britain: Place then the postcode in a new line after the city. That works with if-then conditions. This one adaptation case is sufficient for our exercise, in practice you could of course add further variants in this way.

For this, there is the if-then-else. In plain text:

♦ if country is U.K.,

↳ then add for example city and in following new line postcode,
↳ else city, postcode.

At the Rules button (Mailing's tab), you will find the if-then-else conditions:

➢ Place the cursor in front of the "Contact person" field, then select "If ... Then ... Else" for rules and fill in the following:

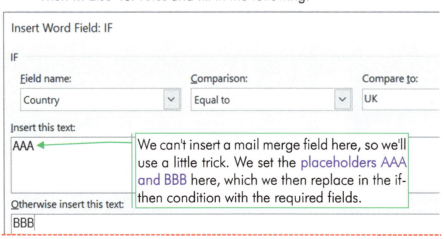

> Right click on the condition, then toggle field codes.

  ↳ Each toggle field codes changes the type of display between result display and condition display.

  ↳ If you press the right mouse button again on if country and toggle field codes, the complete formula is displayed:

{ IF {MERGEFIELD Country} = "UK" "AAA" "BBB"}

Remark: If you click on the right side of the page so that the entire condition line is highlighted, toggle field is sufficient to display the complete condition.

> Now replace AAA with City and BBB with City, Postcode.

> Since we cannot include "new paragraph", just put a similar condition in the following paragraph: if UK, then zip code, nothing else. But the important trick, what empty lines not omitted, add in the if-then-else menu a return direct after postcode without spacebar.

Because this is a little difficult:

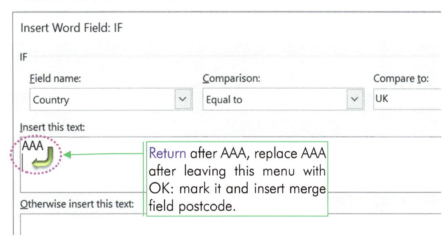

> Finally, just put the country merge field in this line, i.e., delete the paragraph mark beforehand.

Thus, for UK addresses we have the postcode and return, so that Country is in the next line, for all other addresses the postcode is empty here, so that only Country is available, as required without an annoying blank line.

Here are the complete two conditions as illustrative material:

{ IF {MERGEFIELD Country} = "UK" "{MERGEFIELD City}" ""{MERGEFIELD City}, "{MERGEFIELD Postcode}"}

{ IF {MERGEFIELD Country} = "UK" "{MERGEFIELD Postcode} + Return" """"}{MERGEFIELD Country}

Check the result with the preview right away:

Miami, 22222¶
USA¶

Liverpool¶
AK·3AB¶
UK¶

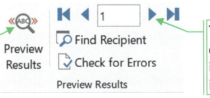

Use this to activate the preview.

Then look at a few data records and check whether the message is only inserted if a contact person is available.

5.6 Display the Field Function

Display the field function *for checking purposes.*

> ➢ Press the right mouse button exactly above the field with the if-else, then toggle field codes. Fist click put on, next off.
>> ✎ You can also use the shortcut [ALT]-F9 to show or hide the field functions, but if you are using a Nvidia graphics card, this shortcut is occupied by a graphics card function for video recording.

[ALT]-F9

Sample for a field function:

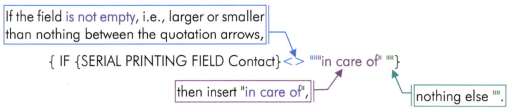

> ➢ Then with the right mouse button again: toggle field codes.

In case you have forgotten the space bar "in care of ", this option is useful for example to add the space bar without having to set the complete if-then condition again.

Insert heading:

> ➢ Now write a headline over the address, very small and formatted in blue:

Delivery address:

This was the delivery bill. We continue with the invoice, where a more difficult condition has to be built in.

5.7 Differentiated Salutation

It's nicer to use the appropriate salutation, Ms for American English and Ms. with dot for British English.

Two steps are necessary to achieve this goal:

This is also intended as an exercise so that you can learn how to use the underlying database.

> ➢ Add a Salutation column in the database, then move the Mr. or Ms. of contact person there.
>> ✎ Also, you can use this field for a Dr or Prof. Dr instead Mr. or Ms.

> ➢ Now correct the salutation to Ms., except for addresses from UK, then enter Ms. with a dot.

> ➢ In the address, now add this new field «Salutation» before the field of Contact Person (right mouse button/toggle field codes, so that you can see it) and please set it up as described

> ➢ and check it again with the preview, e.g., delete some empty paragraph marks so that the invoice follows on the second page.

> ➢ You can also print out a PDF file for testing purposes, e.g., with the "Microsoft print to pdf" printer, and then check this file.

6. The Billing

6.1 Optional Billing Address

An invoice is an invoice. In larger companies the accounting department is often in a different building. Consequently, the address of this department should be on the invoice, and the delivery bill should still show the delivery address.

6.1.1 Add Fields

We need additional fields for the billing address:

- ➢ We have used a copy of the database of sample customers in our exercise folder, just open it like any other Word document.

- ➢ Add new columns for the fields at the end: for address B-Name, B-Street, B-Pcode (for postcode), and B-City.
  - ✍ For this purpose, the field names must be entered as column headers.

- ➢ For some sample addresses, add billing addresses by entering data in the table, you can copy from the file BillAdressesSampleCustomers.

- ➢ Adjust the table format, save and close, then copy the first text field in the invoice document with the address from the delivery bill to the next page to invoice, so we only need to adjust the fields. Delete some empty paragraph marks.

6.1.2 If-Else Invoice address

We now need the following function:

- ◆ If billing address exists, then print billing address, otherwise the normal address.

- ◆ But there is a problem here:
  - ✍ You cannot enter references to other fields in the if-Then-Window but only normal text.

But we still achieve our goal with the same trick. Insert the following If-Then-Else condition as a placeholder.

- ➢ If the mail merge field B-Name is not empty,
  - ✍ then (as placeholder) "then",
  - ✍ else (as placeholder)"else".

The following syntax appears when you select "toggle field codes" with the right mouse button:

{ IF <> " " "then" "else" }

Now we can replace the placeholder text between the quotation marks with the fields:

- ➢ The first quote stitches remain empty.
- ➢ After that, insert the mail merge field B-Name at "then" and (if necessary, again "toggle field codes")
- ➢ for "else otherwise" the mail merge field Name/Company.

Unfortunately, you have to select the "toggle field codes" repeatedly in Word 2019 and in addition, the inserted fields are not displayed.

- ◆ This results in the condition:
  - ↳ If the "B-Name" field is not empty,
  - ↳ then print the "B-Name" field,
  - ↳ else field "Name/Company".

- ➢ This condition still remains if you delete the {Name/Company} field which is now duplicated by copying the entire text field:

{IF {Serial print field B-Name}<> "" "{B-Name}" "{Name/Company}"}

  - ↳ Therefore, if you are looking for help on the if-then-else condition, you must search for "if field" in Word under Help/Help.

- ➢ Test by previewing or printing to a new document.
- ➢ Repeat this procedure for the B-Street, B-Pcode and B-City.

> The invoice address will be printed, if available, otherwise the normal address. Our goal is reached!

6.2 The Calculation

In the invoice, the invoice amount should be calculated and the VAT amount should be indicated as far as possible automatically. Automatic calculations save time and help to avoid calculation errors.

Those who only occasionally need to write invoices, e.g., for a freelance side-line job, and do not want to get used to an accounting program, can make their work in Word easier by using the calculation functions presented here.

The invoice block could be designed in the following way:

INVOICE

Merge field CuNo. and automatic
date via insert/date and time.

Cu.-No.:   «KdNr»
Date: 09/05.11.2024

Description	Unit price	Item	Total price
Microsoft Excel 2021 - Training book with many Exercises: From the Beginning to Advanced Applications, 133 pages, full-color print, ISBN 979-8-849700-86-1	19.90	1	€ 19.90
CorelDRAW 2023 - Training Book with many Exercises, 137 pages, full-color print, ISBN 979-8-858339-52-6	19.90	1	€ 19.90
Corel Photo-Paint 2023: Training Manual with many integrated Exercises, 131 pages, full-color print, ISBN 979-8-862257-62-5	19.90	1	€ 19.90
Microsoft Word 2021 - Second Volume: Training Book with Exercises, 140 pages, full-color print, ISBN 979-8-882701-74-0	19.90	1	€ 19.90
		Sum:	€ 79.60

Discount*:	10 %	€ 7.96
Discount Price:		€ 71,64
Shipping:		€ 6.90
Final amount:		€ 78.54
incl. VAT:	7 %	€ 5.14

Payable within 14 days after the invoice date with 2% discount, payable within 30 days after the invoice date without discount.

We use these Word tools:

♦ The respective article is defined as an AutoText entry (see volume 2), so that it can be entered relatively easily.

♦ The prices are predefined, the quantity will be overwritten if necessary, as long as more than 1.

♦ All other fields, starting from quantity x price, are created as a formula in the table so that the calculation takes place automatically.

 ✎ Right mouse button over formula, update field actualise the result by any changes.

6.2.1 Insert Formula

You can already use AutoText (Insert/QuickParts/AutoText), so here is an explanation of the calculations. We need a product of unit price and quantity, which is on the left, i.e., product (left). It works like this:

> ➢ Place the cursor in the corresponding cell, then:
> Table Tools/Layout/Formula.

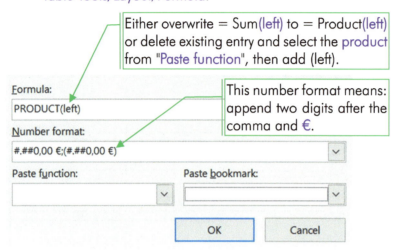

> ➢ You only need to set up the formula once. Simply copy this formula to the following lines.
>
> > ✍ After the first insert, test if you have the formula or just the number, you need to mark the full line to mark the value with the formula.
>
> ➢ Try out: change the quantity of one book, then right mouse button over formula, update field.

6.2.2 Update Fields

You have thus inserted a calculation field. You only need to update if, for example, you want to increase the quantity:

> ➢ Press the right mouse button over the field and select Update Field.
>
> ➢ Proceed in the same way to insert the formula in the last line: Sum(above) in the last line. Do not forget unit €.

Update

6.2.3 A Cross-Reference

Now the sum is taken over into the next table so that there a discount, the value-added tax, and the dispatch portion can be supplemented.

First of all, in principle: why a new table?

> ♦ Calculations in Word only work properly with simple tables.
>
> ♦ Changes in the number of columns can lead to miscalculations.
>
> ♦ Each table field used for calculation must not be empty, but must contain a zero!

However, cross-referencing is not a problem and even a very useful tool. However, before we can set a cross-reference, the value "Sum" must first be defined as a bookmark.

Again, these two steps are necessary:

◆ First, we define as a bookmark what is to be inserted later at another place, e.g., our sum.

◆ Then we can set a cross-reference to this bookmark in the new table.

✎ If the total changes, the current value is entered when you open the document or update the field.

Set bookmarks (as in the chapter about cross-references):

➢ Mark exactly the "Sum" value you just calculated.

➢ Select Insert/Bookmark.

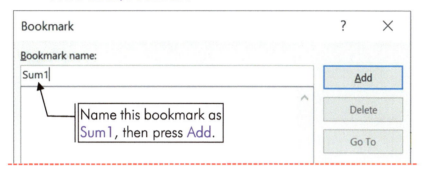

Unfortunately, neither a space bar nor a slash can be used for the name of a bookmark. The Add button is disabled if you have used such characters.

Now, the bookmark is defined and can be inserted in this text as often as you like. This can be done using the Cross-Reference command. We need other bookmarks for our table and the necessary calculations.

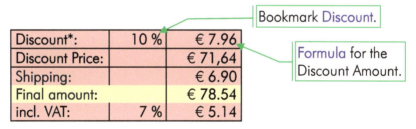

➢ Mark the discount amount 10% and select again: Insert/Bookmark. Define this bookmark as Discount.

Now we can add the formula from the bookmarks Discount and Sum1 to calculate the discount amount:

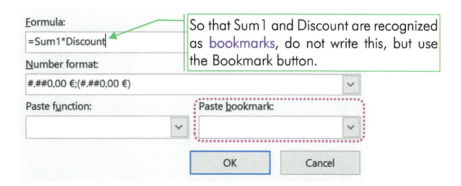

➢ After = at the button "Paste bookmark:" select Sum1, then write * and at "Paste bookmark:" select Discount.

➢ Define the new value as a bookmark DiscountAmount.

➢ If you had also highlighted the %-character for the bookmark Discount, Word correctly calculates 10%, otherwise the formula = Sum1/100* Discount would have to be entered.

> You can enter (almost) any calculation manually, even if there is no predefined function.

Now the other functions are still required:

➢ For the amount with discount: = Sum 1- discount amount.

   ↳ Define this value as a bookmark DiscountPrice

➢ Next row EndAmount + Shipping, manually or you can similar the discount % add a bookmark Shipping and use this in the formula. Mark as FinalAmount.

➢ For the value added tax e.g., by 7% VAT: = FinalAmount/107*VAT. Or you can set a bookmark VAT and use this in the formula.

Overview for the calculation (values are samples):

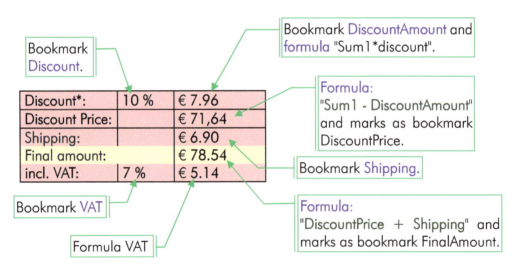

> Bookmarks for VAT, shipping and discounts are helpful when values change, because the entered value is then taken over in the formula when you update the formula.

If you change entries, you may only select the value, not the entire cell, since you would then also overwrite the bookmark.

6.2.4 Recalculate

Because we have built-in some calculations in the meantime, it becomes too cumbersome to update all of them one by one using the right mouse button. It is also not necessary.

This invoice form can be used for any customer by following the steps below:

Start Mail
Merge ▾

- ◆ The ordered articles are inserted as AutoText's, the quantity is corrected and not ordered articles are deleted.
- ◆ Then the amounts are recalculated and the address is inserted with the mail merge function.

> If you change values, you may only select the number, not the whole cell, because you would then overwrite the bookmark.

To overwrite, just click on the value, delete it with [Del] or [Backspace] and rewrite it. In addition, you should set the bookmarks visible in File/Options/-Advanced under header "Show document content".

To update all the fields contained in the document, there is an icon that is best added to the toolbar:

- ➢ File/Options, then select "Quick Access Toolbar" on the left (these are the icons that are displayed at the top left, now only: Save, Undo, Redo).
- ➢ Find the "Update" icon on the left bottom and access the tool bar on the right.

The Result:

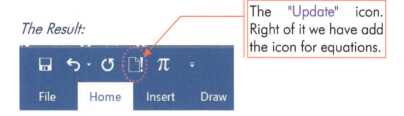

The "Update" icon. Right of it we have add the icon for equations.

Now you can update all calculations very easily:

- ➢ Use [Ctrl]-A to select the entire text.
- ➢ Press the new symbol update or [F9].

[F9]

The terms of delivery and payment are written under the invoice at the end of the process and the bank details are placed in the footer.

6.3 The Customers Query

The invoice is created, what should never be missing is another offer so that every customer can order again. Henceforth, the database is constantly updated and improved, we take this opportunity to ask the customer if his data is correct.

Particular attention can be drawn to missing data.

There are two options that help us again:

♦ We put the data into a textbox again. This prevents the rest of the text from shifting if the addresses are of different lengths.

♦ We insert a condition in each field, for example: if field Phone is empty, then insert text *Your phone?*

This is how the whole thing is supposed to be:

➢ Paste the text and the mail merge fields into a text box as shown.

➢ Set one right-justified tab with fill character so that the rest of the line is underlined.

Is the address correct?
«NameCompany» .... ¶
«Department» .... ¶
«Street» .... ¶
«Postcode» «City» .... ¶
«Contact» .... ¶
Phone: «Phone»? .... ¶
Fax: «Telefax»? .... ¶
Cu.-No.: «CuNo» .... ¶

Now comes the condition:

➢ Place the cursor behind "Phone: "Phone"", then condition of If-Then-Else start. Enter there:

  ↳ If the phone mail merge field is empty, then: "Your phone? "

  ↳ "Otherwise insert this text": leave blank or set a placeholder e.g., PPP and replace this with the merge field Phone, so the customer sees his actual phone number and can check if ok.

➢ Format the inserted condition "Your phone? " in italics, bold and with Color Red to make it clearly visible. If the condition is not visible, switch the field function on/off (toggle field codes).

➢ Copy the condition for the other fields: Fax, street, contact, etc., then modify the text.

➢ Perform a Test with the first data set   .

Formulas once defined can be copied:

Mark the number (note the grey background that indicates the field), copy it and paste it elsewhere. Use the right mouse button to select the Update Field command, so that the amount is correct.

7. Shortcuts

7.1 Standard-Shortcuts

[Ctrl]-n	New Text	[Ctrl]-x	Cut out
[Ctrl]-o	Open Text	[Ctrl]-c	Copy
[Ctrl]-s	Save	[Ctrl]-v	Paste
[Ctrl]-p	Open Print menu.	F1 oder ?	Help
[Ctrl]-z	Undo		

7.2 Selected Shortcuts for longer Texts

[Ctrl]-[Pos 1]	To the beginning.
[Ctrl]-[End]	To the end of the Text.
[Ctrl]-[Return]	Insert page break.
[Ctrl]-Hyphen	Manual Hyphenation.
Select:	
[Shift] - Direction keys - Image buttons	Select (from the Current Cursor Position).
[Ctrl]-[Shift] -[Pos 1] / -[End]	To select from the current cursor position to the beginning or end of the text.
[Ctrl]-a	Select all.
Important Windows:	
[Ctrl]-g	Opens the Go-To window.
[Ctrl]-f	Opens the Search Window.
[Ctrl]-h	Opens the Replace Window.
Style sheets:	
[Ctrl]-[Alt]-[Shift]-s	Opens the Styles menu.

7.3 Additional Shortcuts

Finally, we have printed a selection of Shortcuts. You can find a complete compilation in the Help of MS Word.

Select the Function keys:

F1   Help
F4   Repeat the previous operation
F5   Select the Go to command
F7   Selecting the Spelling command (Check menu)
F8   Expand selection: you can select the word first, then the paragraph, the paragraph including Paragraph Selection and the whole document by pressing [F8] several times. Switch off again with [Esc].
F9   Update Fields Selection
F12   Select the Save As command

Select Combinations with the [Shift] key:

SHIFT-F3   Changing the upper/lower case character of the letters
SHIFT-F4   Repeat Searches or Go to

Useful combinations with the [Ctrl] and [Shift] keys:

CTRL-SHIFT-F5   Edit a Bookmark
CTRL-SHIFT-F6   Go to the previous Window
CTRL-SHIFT-F7   Update linked data in a Microsoft Word source document
CTRL-SHIFT-F8   select in rectangular form (then press the arrow keys)
CTRL-SHIFT-F9   Cancel a Field Link

Select Combinations with the [Alt] key:

ALT-F1   Go to next Field
ALT-F3   Create an AutoText Entry (text must be selected)
ALT-F4   Exit Microsoft Word
ALT-F7   Find the next spelling or grammar error
ALT-F8   the Macro-Window appears from which a Macro can be started.
ALT-F9   Toggles between Field function/Result for all Fields
ALT-F10   a window appears in which all graphic elements of the current page are displayed. By clicking on the eye, an element can be made invisible.
ALT-F11   View the Microsoft Visual Basic code. This window can easily be closed again with the X symbol.

Reference: MS Word Help, search for "key combinations" at the bottom of the list. Here you will find a list of all available shortcuts.

8. Index